Praise for *Retiren*

Retirement is a subject ma... is that the readings are extremely dull and 'same old, same old.' This book is anything but dull, old, and repetitive. It breaks the mold on how to retire successfully. I think Bill has hit the sweet spot regarding thriving in retirement. I join Bill in support of the eight DNA elements and themes. His stories and experiences are brilliant. This book will do well; this book will sell because it's unique. Go, Bill, go! —*John Cheng, a.k.a. White Pepper — Semi-retired businessmen in the Asian food and beverage industry.*

Retirement can be your 'golden years' which you truly enjoy, or your 'tarnished years' which you feel are miserable and lost! I think the DNA of retirement is a comprehensive guide that will help many prepare for this autumn season of life and to live it well. The book promises the life adventure of being funny, entertaining, helpful, and timely. So don't miss out the surreal journey of a retiree. —*Eddie Chan – Executive Director of the Association of Accredited Advertising, Singapore. Retired 2005.*

What does a dog do in retirement? He doesn't lie around; that was his job. In his latest book, old dog Bill is not lying around as he offers a humorous take on retirement. After reading the book, I realized that the biggest problem with retirement is that you don't get a day off — too many cats to chase, bones to bury, and life to live. Bill may have to go back to his old job to get a rest. —*Susan P. Oliver — Theatrical Producer, Director, and Actress. Retired 2000.*

'Retirement' is a misdemeanor or a word that is inappropriate. It is perceived by non-retirees as if your 'working life' is over; how incorrect is this! Bill hits the nail on the head with insights, stories, and the way to move forward to have a really exciting last third of your life. The song from the Carpenters springs to mind 'We've only just begun...' The most significant awareness for me is that I have become wiser, more tolerant, a better listener, and more worldly since retiring. Bill has done a great job depicting this way of being. Thriving in a surreal world is living your dreams. Bill shows us the way to do this. —*Patrick Percey — National Business Manager /National Sales & Distribution Manager, Levi Strauss Australia. Retired 2002.*

I've known Billy Peace since 1965. Even then he paved his own way, stood by what he knew to be true, offered a smile at every turn, and held close to his friends. In his book he stays true to these attributes and even writes like he speaks — full of positive energy. Amidst the bumps along the way that life always offers, his drive to make a difference in both small and large ways, while enjoying simple moments and taking complex projects to completion, continues to inspire! Keep going, Billy, you are nailing it! His book reinforces my fun life, taking on many new things, reinventing myself. Like ceramic sculpturing, swimming and working out at the gym, being a practicing Reiki master teacher, mentoring with a great coach, and moving toward a PhD, just for the heck of it. —*C. Bean — Manager, Department of Mental Health, Youth Services, Adult Rehabilitation, and Corrections, State of Ohio. Retired 2012.*

Bill provides a unique and refreshing view into the world of retirement. Bill's 'retirement' in real life was but another journey in his long and successful career. His observations and learnings along the way are very well depicted in *Retirement: The Surreal Life Adventure*. This is a must read for anyone starting their own retirement journey. —*Glen Prasser — CEO, Beacon Orthopedics & Sports Medicine. Retired 2016. Previously, Associate Director, Global Supply Chain, Procter & Gamble. Retired 2008.*

Retirement to me is NOT looking back and asking WHY? It is looking forward and asking WHY NOT? Bill's book is right on target, looking at and living possibilities for a thriving new life. I recommend the book to anyone who is interested in living a surreal retirement. When one door of happiness closes (like my 34 and 1/2-year career with ExxonMobil) another door opens (for retirement). But often we spend so long looking at the closed door that we do not see the one which has been opened for us to enjoy. Life's circumstances are not always what you might wish them to be. Rather than wandering about or questioning the direction your life has taken, accept the fact that here is a path before you now — *Retirement: The Surreal Life Adventure.* —*Timothy Kevin Callery — Managing Director, ExxonMobil. Retired 2007.*

Retirement: The Surreal Life Adventure

© 2016 by William D. Peace, Jr.
Illustrations by Trinuch Chareon
All rights reserved.

Published by Mission Point Press
2554 Chandler Lake Road,
Traverse City, MI, 49696

MissionPointPress.com

No part of this book may be reproduced, stored in a retrieval system, or transmitted in any form or by any means electronic, mechanical, photocopying, recording or otherwise, without the prior consent of the publisher.

ISBN: 978-1-943995-18-9

Library of Congress Control Number: 2016915225

Printed in the United States of America.

RETIREMENT
THE SURREAL LIFE ADVENTURE

WILLIAM D. PEACE, JR.
AUTHOR OF "SUPPLY CHAIN MANAGEMENT: THE REAL WOW FACTOR"

MISSION POINT PRESS

TABLE OF CONTENTS

Dedication ... 9

Introduction ... 11

The DNA of Retirement Life:
Way of Being ... 13

Lifestyle ... 33

Physical ... 55

Mental ... 73

Emotional ... 97

Family and Friends ... 117

Spiritual ... 133

Financial ... 151

Interviews with the Over 60s Folks ... 165

The Mantra ... 175

That Which Says It All ... 177

About the Author ... 178

DEDICATION

I dedicate this book to my Thai father-in-law who lived life large before and after retiring from the car industry in 2005.

Since being with him for over 12 years, he inspired me to retire gracefully, live life to the fullest, and give back joy to the world.

Most people struggle in retirement — not him, he embraced it through his love of life, positive attitude, sheer happiness, and engagement with and commitment to the people he loved, all over the world.

I was blessed to be one of those people he cared about. When I retired in 2007 he took me under his wing, taught me how to get the most out of retirement, and live life with no regrets.

I kept an active journal on the subject of what I learned from him and experienced with him.

Hence this book, *Retirement: The Surreal Life Adventure*. ENJOY, CELEBRATE!

INTRODUCTION

This book is not your normal politically correct, self-help book on retirement. It is not a result of countless readings on the subject nor attending seminars on preparing for and surviving in retirement. Most of the norms and "to-do's" read or heard did not work for me. They were boring, mundane, cliché, and not fun. For example: go to the gym every day; eat whole grain foods; grow old gracefully (What? No fun element?); drink cranberry juice; learn a new set of skills (What? As if the skills you've acquired your whole life aren't good enough.); don't eat red meat (What? My healthy 93-year-old dad eats red meat.); go to bed early/wake up early (What? You've been doing this your whole working life). No thanks.

I have experienced a whole new, exciting, and surreal retirement the last nine years since leaving a very large multi-national company after 32 years at the grindstone. Is there life after work? You bet and it's wonderful. You can thrive instead of just survive … but only, for the most part, if you follow elements of the DNA of life in this book that work for you. It contains a different collection of success elements served up to invigorate and inspire you so that you can spend the rest of your life in bliss versus lament. I suggest you read the collection of elements and try on/use what works for you. Like shopping for clothes, some will fit and some won't.

As a footnote Wikipedia defines "surreal" as: having the quality of a dream, having the characteristics of surrealism, unreal, fantastic, and bizarre. Experience *Retirement: The Surreal Life Adventure* and think about the possibility that this could be the new normal for you. Have you had your surreal life adventure today? Your S.L.A.?

THE DNA
OF RETIREMENT LIFE:

WAY OF BEING

*You are older and wiser now.
Don't do activities like eating contests,
extreme sports, or bungee jumping.*

A lot of people are concentrating on therapeutic activities. Men are spending all day fixing and painting lamps — handyman stuff. Women are spending more time pruning trees and gardening. Your kids love having you over to do all the odd jobs. This provides a chance for gentle bonding and shared learning.

*If you are not spending at least one morning
or afternoon a week at an outside café
watching people go by, then you are either
too busy or have missed the point
of retirement bliss completely.*

One of the biggest decisions you'll have to make is whether to have an iced or hot latte. If you don't do too much, then the time will pass more slowly, which is a good thing. But it's phenomenal how fast the time does go by in retirement. I guess it's because we are having so much fun.

Only do one big activity per day.

If you're too busy, time passes more quickly and you only have a third of your life left. A great phenomenon is that about five years after you retire everyone thinks you look great and even younger. This is a result of no stress by not cramming too much into the day.

*If you complete a life plan before retirement,
you probably accomplished it all
in the first year.*

Now just sit back and relax. Doing absolutely nothing is OK once in a while. A colleague put it in perspective for me. He was always asked what he would do now that he had retired. His response, "I really don't know what I'm going to do, and I'm not worried about it. Right now I'm retired and relaxed. If and when it becomes a problem, I'll figure it out."

Don't criticize people who, under a doctor's care, experiment with medical marijuana.

Maybe they are just living their college days again. Regarding doctors, notice that you will rely on them more frequently to help you extend and maybe even save your life. Make sure they understand your expectation on this — you're the customer and they're the supplier. No more doctor visits whereby he or she says, "You're schizophrenic." You say, "I want a second opinion." The doctor says, "You're ugly too."

One possible mantra in retirement could be: "If I could party all night and sleep all day and throw all my problems away, my life would be easy!" (adopted from the Black Eyed Peas).

But please keep a good balance in your way of being. Retirees have a huge responsibility to be responsible. People look up to you — behave.

There is a reason your kids and grandkids laugh at you for the long "to-do lists" on the refrigerator.

Cut it in half; you're retired now. I like the way my sister puts it, "What does a dog do on his day off? He doesn't lie around, that's his job. I realize that the biggest problem with retirement is that you don't get a day off — too many cats to chase, bones to bury, and life to live."

Never ever live in a boring town again.

If you do then revert back to the normal, boring coaching you received for retirement: learn new skills, go to the gym daily, never stop working, and so forth because you will have the time to do these survival things. Plus, your kids won't visit you — too boring, no fun. Thrive in an exciting place. Two guys are sitting in the airport lounge, one says to the other, "Hey, where are you from?" The other guy says, "St. Paul Minnesota, very boring and full of hookers and hockey players." Whereby the first guy says, "My wife's from St. Paul." The response, "Really, what position did she play?"

Don't get coerced into lots of sight-seeing. You've seen enough. Don't do anything you really don't want to do.

I'm sure you've noticed retirees on vacation with family and friends sitting by the pool reading a book or in a park feeding the birds while their mates are visiting monuments, going to museums and theme parks. Been there, done that, bought the t-shirt.

*Spend time observing people
and the world around you.*

That is assuming this is something you did not do while working. And silence is good. Remember after work when your ears were ringing from all the cacophony in the workplace? A retired Thai executive put it this way, "I have been a watcher of people around me seeing them grow or dwindle, laugh or cry. As a watcher of people, I reflectively watch myself from time to time. Such exercises keep me in balance."

*Guys, savor a good cigar once in a while.
Gals, have the occasional Virginia Slims
or cigar if you want to.*

Make it last a long time because that's what you have—time. Across the street in our neighborhood growing up, we would watch in amazement as our retired medical doctor rode around on his riding mower, very slowly mowing his lawn, enjoying his pipe — probably using up no less than half of his tobacco in one sitting. As my high school class of '71 buddies look back on this, they wondered if maybe it was medical marijuana. Here's a smoking oddity: on airplanes retirees know that smoking has been banned for over 25 years and yet they still produce planes with the no smoking icon above every seat. You'd think we all get it by now, right?

A good time is watching your retirement home perimeter lights come on at precisely the same time every night.

Regarding your way of being, get in a Zen mood, relax, and watch the auto-electric lights do their thing. An Asian buddy of mine, now retired, came to stay with us on Phuket. He sat on the deck, started to hum in a meditative state, watched the sun go down, and then the 40 wall lights came on. He asserted, "That's bliss, great karma, and definitely good feng shui." You can get a double fantasy if you get up in the morning and watch the automatic sprinklers come on at exactly the same time every day. Amazing how little things in life give you just the right endorphin rush — in your thriving retirement years.

*Put off today what you can
always do tomorrow.*

Find a balance of busy and non-busy, let time flow, don't dictate time. Even a weekly to-do list can be put off until next week. What's amusing is to watch how impatient your working spouse becomes at some delays in your house-spouse or man-nanny (Manny) list. Oh well. They will understand when they retire.

Live in a warm climate.

Your blood thins. Jackets are even required in northern Michigan, Florida, or Arizona in the summer evenings, especially for Asians and South Americans. A very close colleague got a twofer; he retired from a large multi-national company while living in dire straits locations, and relocated to Puerto Rico to work for the Bacardi Rum Company. He had the best of both worlds — a warm climate and the frequent, refreshing free beverage.

Know that your memory will fade.

List things to do inside and outside the house, what to buy, what errands to run, what work and fun things to do. Just don't put the lists on the refrigerator for your kids to laugh at. One of the phenomenon you might experience is this: think of something you have to do in one room in the house, go out to do it, forget what it was, then go back to the original room where you got the thought and it comes back. An elderly husband is asked by his wife to go to the kitchen to get her vanilla ice cream with strawberries. He comes back with chocolate ice cream and peaches. Go figure, she says;, "Hey, I wanted toast with my bacon and eggs."

Be the caretaker of your winter and summer places, but hire everything out.

Do minimum yard work. If you have to move, then hire it out. Splurge on a pickup truck or a refurbished POS (piece of s**t), but hire out the maintenance and refurbishments. This brings up one of the greatest skills you will pick up in retirement: being an orchestrator. Get to know the hand movements when coaching your help.

Enjoy boredom every once in a while.

You've been a human doing all your working life, now be a human being. You wouldn't be the first person who says, "I'm not lazy. I just choose to do nothing every once in a while." A semi-retired UK friend of mine lives on a remote island in Indonesia. He got bored once and bought a very expensive remote control power boat to play with, sent it out to sea, lost the range and never saw it again. Not to become discouraged, he bought a very expensive drone with GPS and a very expensive camera on board. His video showed it was following boats on a canal and watching golfers on his course. The last scene showed the drone crashing into the jungle. Unsalvageable. He's back to being bored every once in a while as his way of being.

LIFESTYLE

Never eat what you don't want to eat.

Take over the kitchen, learn to cook, then you will surely eat only what you truly want. Plus, in retirement there are no longer set times for breakfast, lunch, and dinner. No more planned schedules anymore. Lots of retirees are reinventing themselves and are learning or re-learning to cook — it's therapeutic. With no timetable, it no longer matters how long a cake takes to bake.

*Keep plenty of shorts, jeans,
and polo shirts in your closet.*

Wear bathing suits and cut-off shorts a lot. A t-shirt can be the dress of the day. And, you don't have to buy anymore new clothes — your existing ones will probably outlast you anyway. Old clothes feel better as well. You must tell your relatives that you no longer need a new tie, polo shirt, or shorts. No more new bags, shoes, watches, and jewelry either as that stuff for sure will outlast you.

Never wake up before 9 a.m.

You had to wake up early most of your life for kids, work, travel, etc. It's beyond comprehension why some retirees schedule a weekly 8 a.m. breakfast or a Saturday 8 a.m. book club session. Also daily power naps are good, as sleep becomes a virtue in retirement The jury is still out on the idea of whether it's important to shower before noon.

Stay up really late if you want to.

The limit might be 2 a.m. at your age, unless you're having a great time. Staying up past 10 can be very productive as there are often no disturbances, great late-night TV, and some quiet time from the hustle and bustle. Activities abound such as catching up on missed prime-time reality TV shows like "Junior Master Chef," "Scandal," "Anthony Bourdain," and "American Idol." You might have to explain to your working spouse why this is good for you.

*Enjoy ice lattes with whole milk and
real sugar every once in a while.*

Perfect in the morning while your spouse, family, or friends go shopping or site-seeing. An email was floating around recently about having lunch with a 75-year-old. The gentleman ordered a piece of pie with two scoops of ice cream. The waitress asked, "How come you always order rich desserts for lunch?" Whereupon the gentleman responded, "I'm tasting all that is possible for me to taste. I try to eat the food I need and do the things I should in order to stay healthy, but life's too short. I hate missing out on something good. This year I realized how old I was, so while I'm still here, I've decided it's time to try all those things that, for years, I've been ignoring."

Always keep your wine rack full.

Consider it a great project. We all know people who have transformed their basement into a wine cellar. There's a guy here in Singapore who has transformed the second biggest bedroom in his apartment into a wine cellar. And he's American — go figure. Bar-b-que often. And cleaning it pristinely can also be a good project. In retirement euphoria, you now have time to really entertain.

Eat donuts, ice cream, and candy when you want to.

Another phenomenon is how your sense of taste will improve exponentially — compensating for the slight loss of hearing, memory, and eyesight. Speaking of various food groups, be cautious of retirement periodicals and newsletters that claim some very dodgy things. One such retirement newsletter author claims that drinking three cups of coffee per day will eliminate cancer. Apparently that's what he does. The same gent professes that only extra virgin olive oil will improve your health, not the normal kind, but advises not to burn it while cooking. For real? Not.

If you drink, have never more than three categories.

This means like beer, wine, and scotch. Enjoy drinks with friends and never drink alone. Shots are off the list as well. No more, "Hey, daddy, I'm 21, I think I'll have 21 shots of tequila!" Take homage and learn the lesson to stay moderately balanced. A recently, semi-retired Scottish friend of mine takes his very responsible wife to the pub with him. If not, he indulges in way too many beverages, forgets to pay the bill, and walks to the nearby taxi stand without his shoes on.

No more fruity cocktails and no more drinks with umbrellas in them.

This practice is bad for the older and wiser image. Take direction from the well-seasoned retired people who still have cocktail parties. The beverages of choice are scotch, gin, vodka, wine, and beer — no fruity drinks like Singapore Slings or Mai Tais. A very special woman in northern Michigan was a great entertainer, lived to be 100, and recalled that, for her, alcohol was a preservative.

Achieve a 12 or better handicap in golf.

I'm sure you did before you worked full time for a living. It's remarkable how handicaps plunge when retired. For instance, 80-year-old women are winning on Woman's Day. Case in point, my mother. I believe it was when my father was 88 I first beat him at golf, much to his embarrassment, particularly when his old buddies in the cart behind us found out — what a cacophony. In a very sleepy little town in southern Michigan, a very prominent Monsignor from the Catholic Church retired, hooked up with the local golf pro, played three times a week, and frequented the local pub where several beverages were consumed. You get the picture. A new bartender asked one of the patrons, "How did he ever get the nickname, Monsignor?"

Play drums to stay limber, or an electric guitar, or any other musical instrument that you've craved to play.

And play loudly regardless of the fact that you do not have a hearing problem as you age. The new rage across the world with old people is music therapy; playing an instrument, dancing, and playing any kind of music. This accesses the endorphins and dopamine that we all need. Thriving in retirement is talking to friends about the good old times — the best guitars, playing drums or singing in rock and blues bands in the '60s and '70s, seeing Jimi Hendrix set his guitar on fire in Cleveland in 1967. Most of us regret giving away our Tama drums or the classic Stratocaster guitar to our kids.

Never again take morning flights.

You have to get up way too early for these flights. Let go of the 9 to 5 thing. Adjust to your new time schedule, consider it an internal control vs. external, working-life control. Anyway, you know airports aren't fun in the mornings — too many grumpy, tired, hacked-off people. The afternoon is so much better — happy people, end of the day letting loose, great food and shopping experiences, and the occasional beverage. If you happen to be in Changi Airport in Singapore, voted the world's best airport four years running, you'll find it's a party after 5 p.m.

Face it, the days of business class travel are over.

Get used to economy. Your work-accumulated airline miles will run out before you do. This is not a bad thing, by the way. There's always premium economy. It is a little embarrassing if the crew knows you from the working days and sees you in less-than-business class. No worries, you're still respected as being older and wiser. They often look up to you and may give you a free upgrade.

Only wear socks if you plan to wear sneakers.

White socks with loafers is old school. Your kids and the new generations will definitely make fun of you. But it was cool in our day. It's one thing to be respected in retirement, being older and wiser, it's completely another (bad) thing to look like a complete out-of-touch idiot. This may be a transformation for some of us if extreme sports aren't on the agenda anymore, which require socks and sneakers. Instead, sandals might be the footwear of the day.

Really get to love grocery shopping.

Many retirees, whose spouse or significant other is still working and on-the-go, enjoy being a nanny or man-nanny (Manny) or house spouse. They love doing the grocery shopping, having the house cleaned (hired out, of course), managing the finances, and paying the bills. It's a full-time job for any man or woman. At least as far as shopping goes, men go in the store, find what they want and get out; the straight-line approach so they have more time during the day to just chill. For women, it could take up the whole day browsing every aisle.

Never watch sitcoms again.

Say yes to reality TV. During the day you can watch the live trials of notorious folks like Anna Nicole-Smith, O.J. Simpson, or Oscar Pistorius — great fun, that. Night time provides a double bonus. Go home early to avoid partying all night with your younger friends and catch the latest thrilling episodes of "Cake Boss," "Project Runway," and "Asia's Next Top Model." All could be part of a thriving lifestyle for you.

As you will be cooking more, possibly a new skill set for you, get into a weekly regimen.

Like beef, chicken, pork, fish, then go out to dinner for what possibly could be stress relief. If cooking isn't your thing, or if it's all you've ever done, then go out to dinner often. Take precautionary measures if you splurge too much for lunch and/or dinner. Do the yin and yang thing: a little more exercise, a little more sleep, or a little less food the next day.

It's OK to leave dishes in the sink overnight.

During your working life as a Type A personality human-doer this would be out of the question. Right? Be careful if your spouse still works. This could drive him/her completely nuts. Choose the moment when dishes need to be done, like when your spouse rants on about the workday. Doing the dishes could be a good distraction.

Keep your bike well-greased and shiny.

Do this whether you ride it or not, depending on your doctor's advice. If it's in good shape, your family and friends will be impressed. If riding becomes too stressful on your limbs then the stationary bike can be the vehicle of choice, albeit you don't get anywhere. Worldwide, the next evolution as aging continues is the electric, sit-down three-wheeler — the technology on these things is incredible. However, racing might be out of the question and three-wheeling certainly will not become an Olympic sport.

PHYSICAL

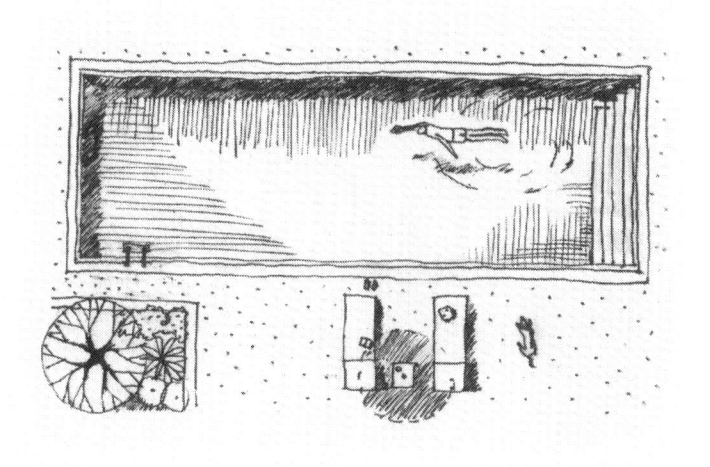

Now, as opposed to when you were working, you will have three priorities.

They are eating well, sleeping well, and exercising without injuring yourself. Successful people create a balance, an equilibrium. Again, if you eat too well and sleep too well, then exercise more. If you exercise too much and you wonder why your legs are throbbing, then sleep or relax more. Create the right rhythm. Drinking lots of pure water has been a suggestion. But note that Evian spelled backwards is Naïve. Come on. Just boil water, cool it, and pour it into your favorite container.

Sell or donate your extreme sports gear.

This could include scuba equipment, snow skis, hang glider, dirt bike, snow mobile, etc. Then there's the new rage: paddle boarding. Kids, grandkids, young adults, the millennials — all find this very soothing, relaxing, and great fun paddling upright and stoically on various bodies of water around the world. Dogs and small babies are now taking a ride. That's crazy, and dangerous. Having tried it with the young ones, I find it an extreme sport. "No, my second darling daughter, I will not buy you one of these silly, boring, unstable, bad-on-the-knees, senseless things. I don't want you to get hurt like I did during my first time on one." For the record, and much to the dismay of my children, I call the sport "water boarding."

Learn to fish again.

It's a great passive, relaxing, time-consuming sport. But no more extreme trips to Canada where you have to camp on an island due to the recent bear attacks. Use a rowboat — nothing fast and furious. Grandkids, nieces, nephews, and all small children love to go fishing with you. It's good bonding time and you might get a bonus when an otter steals your bait. My nephew pee'd his pants when this actually happened to him.

Your blood will thin.

Especially if you winter in a warm climate and return to a cool summer up north. Wear a coat to the next bonfire. Yes, people will make fun of you but it's all part of the retirement experience, right? Realize that it's not just retirees;. As mentioned, thin-blooded Asians and South Americans visit America in the summer, and they wear coats all the time, day and night.

Live life in moderation, but not too much.

The human species subscribes to a "live-all-out" phenomenon. There are workaholics, shopaholics, fitnessaholics, sleepaholics, foodaholics, and yes, alcoholics. Why do we live this way? Retirement is your chance to break the morass. And it's not just in the physical DNA element of life but in others: lifestyle, mental, emotional, and family and friends. For example, pertaining to our physical DNA element, it's why a strong commitment to sell all your extreme sports gear is wise. My father when he was 75 years old went downhill skiing and guess what, he broke his thumb. How silly and how lucky he was.

Don't try new and exotic foods.

It's not worth the heartburn. Always taste first before diving in. And it's not embarrassing to ask for minimum spice in Thai or Indian food. Now's the time in your life to eat food you need and want. Abandon the rule that you should always eat what's put in front of you — OK during your upbringing, not OK in your new life. And remember, now as opposed to your younger years, it's OK to have cake for lunch or dinner.

Don't pick up any new hobbies.

You already have enough. You really don't need to learn anything new either. From decades of working, our brains are already full. Having said this, retired women around the world seem to reinvent themselves more than men by being far more skilled on the internet, setting up companies via the web, maneuvering online buying, and other current new-age rages. On the other hand, a very successful MNC executive retired recently, only to get bombarded with, "You must learn new things to keep your mind active, and you must pick up new activities to stay physically and mentally challenged." His response, "Why? I'm full-up already." Having said this he is working with World Vision of Thailand, helping build schools for poor kids all over Asia. This is not a hobby, and he didn't have to learn anything new to do this noble endeavor.

Getting really fit is no longer on your "to-do list." Being fit enough will do.

Again, everything in moderation. Retirees who thrive always remind themselves that professional athletes only have a mortality rate of 55 years — not good. If you are getting hounded to go to the gym, then call the John (bathroom), the Jim. "Hey, I'm going to the Jim every day, sometimes twice." And, if you are getting hounded for not taking invigorating walks, then name your dog "5 Miles." You can say, "Hey, I walk 5 Miles every day, often twice a day."

Losing weight or gaining weight are also not on your "to-do list."

Some of us were really skinny growing up. Duh, we ran around a lot, played outdoors. Working 10 hours a day without much food didn't help either. Now, in retirement bliss, of course we slow down, look healthier, gain a few pounds. Have you been told chubby is the new skinny? I have, by my oldest daughter. The good news is currently the world's obesity problem is not directed toward retirees. The bad news is even the once Third World nations like China and India are facing the problem — particularly with the young. Do you think it has something to do with the internet and gadget age? And another thing, why is it when you retire, people bug you about losing or gaining weight? A little late, don't you think? You're not going to be a contestant on the "Bachelor" or "Bachelorette" show anyway.

If and/or when you exercise, don't do anything that causes you to sweat.

Get a motorized standup scooter. Much easier on the arthritic knees than a bike, and they now come with seats. It's inspirational seeing an 80-year-old lady scooting down the sidewalk and all over town on one of these. If you live in a big city they are the best alternative to horrible taxi rides. You know those rides: drunk drivers, or fidgeting ones who cause the cab to jump, or even the ones who know where you're from and try to mimic your accent! The worst taxi ride is when there are exotic, clicking bobble-head figures in the back window that make you feel like a tarantula spider is about to land on your shoulder.

Losing hair? Enjoy seeing more of your skin.

A natural phenomenon is that you always have been losing your hair — you just didn't have time to notice it. And, guys, what's wrong with the Yul Brynner look? It can be part of the older and wiser shtick. You're enjoying life more now — who has time for haircuts? Just shave it clean and polish it often, another great project during retirement. Getting gray? Then enjoy nicknames like the silver fox, white pepper, gray ghost, and the gray widow.

Guys, grow your hair long, get the look back that you had in the '70s.

Grow a ponytail, especially if you've grayed. Many of us know guys in their 70s, 80s and 90s who do this. Like my old relive-the-70s Uncle Ned, who put his long, gray hair in a ponytail, lived up north in the summer, hopped in his beat-up old car and sold knickknacks and antiques on the way to the Florida Keys in the winter. Oh yes, and never dye your hair unless you live in Asia where black hair is a must all your life until the end. Have you ever wondered why Asians do not want dark skin? It's because they think it looks dirty, yet black hair is the must-have cultural experience! Gals, get a pageboy again. To go with your occasional Virginia Slim.

Remember during your working days the toe tapping, heel tapping, and leg bouncing?

Relief! These skill sets are no longer needed. Fidgeting, excessive energy spurts, and nervousness are no longer part of your DNA. Notice this stops automatically when you retire — a true phenomenon. A quadruple fantasy: your legs and knees feel better, you are more calm, you are less noisy with friends, and your fingernails grow out. What's fun now is reminiscing about the old days by watching the working-folk leg bounce and fidget like a dog who plays air guitar when you scratch his belly.

Avoid too much walking around.

Take a bus or a cab. And never ever run for a bus, taxi or train again. You have time to catch the next one. Light walking or jogging is OK, for short distances, and under the direction of your doctor. Running is a controversial subject. Shin splints, sore knees, and being humiliated by your younger partner who is way ahead all the time can do harm — physically and mentally. The March, 2016, "Men's Health" publication ran a serious advertisement showing a runner propped up against a street wall. It read, "What to do if you get diarrhea while running. You've probably experienced the need to poop halfway through the run. That's because the physical motion of running manhandles your intestines...but there is a way to prevent that, visit www.blahblahblah.com." Really? Don't run.

Growing older means more ear and nose hair, unwanted mustaches and chin hair — not to mention hairy eyebrows.

It's best to trim often. Epilators are too painful and the hair grows back anyway, a retiree's dilemma. Be positive and let this quirk be part of the more sophisticated physical way of being. Hearing can possibly be an issue. But before you go for tests or run out for a hearing aid, take heed; generally speaking, around the world, people are mumbling and speaking more quietly, with less certainty, than they used to. The art of language has been compromised. There is a theory going around that the internet age of emails, texting, SMS-ing, WhatsApp-ing, etc., our new forms of communication, has caused this phenomenon. We have lost our ability to speak and communicate clearly. Everyone is asking everyone to repeat themselves. So, oh thriving retiree, before you panic, see if you have noticed this of late and don't sweat a hearing problem.

Never lift or carry anything heavy again.

Leave this activity to the younger generations. Face it, your body is more frail and less agile. I can never understand why 80- and 90-year-olds are trying to act out life like a 40- or 50-year-old. The days of manhandling a chain saw or moving heavy boxes (at 80 years old) are over. You get clued in when you realize 40- and 50-year-olds aren't breaking their hips all the time, but 80- and 90-year-olds are. Take homage, no more of this "Me Tarzan, you Jane."

MENTAL

Get a sponsor, mentor, and/or coach to keep from wandering aimlessly.

You will miss having a good boss or a good leader who helped you during the working days. And it doesn't mean getting a mother or father figure — been there, done that. Notice thriving retirees hanging out with friends 20 years younger. They are known to be great coaches on how to feel young again. I have one who coaxed me into buying a standup electric scooter — quite fun, that, and I didn't need a seat.

*If you just have to learn something new,
then learn patience.*

This is something you never had time for while you were working. Patient people are calm, they listen well, and see and hear things that others don't. A famous philosopher, Marcel Proust, once said, "Adventure is not in new landscapes, but seeing things through different eyes." Patient people understand this. Just make sure your glasses prescription is up-to-date.

A good day is not getting lost in the mall and feeling stupid.

Nowadays, malls are becoming more like labyrinths. I think the developers want you to get lost so you will see more shops to possibly buy something. Don't take it personally; even the young ones get lost in malls, particularly here in Asia. Ask the information desk person where the shop you're looking for is, which is a bonus since you now have someone to talk to.

Learn to say "no."

This is something in your work skill-set that was previously nonexistent. Start out practicing with your dog, "Whiteshoes, no, no, you can't come into the house." You live now with internal control versus external control. The freedom of "no" can be exhilarating. When you do volunteer work like tutoring or teaching English, be cautious. The parents may try to coax you back to the days of work/work, "Oh please, just three more sessions this week?" You reply, "Boom-done for the week." Success.

Always be in a mental state of authority.

Retired people of authority, and prominent people in the community are fortunate enough to have some great jobs available to them. The positions that come to mind are: greeters at church, committee leaders, fund-raisers, and even Walmart greeters. And you certainly don't need to learn any new skills for these jobs. As far as authority is concerned, a retired bar owner in Thailand exercises this a little too much when he often travels away and tells his staff to run everything. Not too difficult in the Western world, but in the developing countries it's tough. Locals running a bar or restaurant without guidance, and the absence of authority, can be chaos.

Never be bored waiting in line.

Use the time to meditate, get into a mental Zen state of being — even pray. It's a great opportunity for observing things and people around you. You can be entertained and amused watching everyone fidgeting nervously, and checking the time on their smartphones every few seconds. Celebrate, you are finally under no time pressure. Such bliss.

*Believe that work
is no longer a four-letter word.*

Any type of work in retirement should be fun. And remember, you can control this versus others. Maybe retirement should be called re-toolment. In the words of Monty Python, "And now for something completely different." Fun work.

Now you can read constantly for enjoyment.

This doesn't mean emails, Twitter, WhatsApp, or Facebook incessantly. Try reading books, magazines, and newspapers that get your hands inky — reminiscent of the earlier days. "Old school" can be the "new school." This can be rediscovering fun and setting off the enjoyable endorphin and dopamine rushes in your brain. Guaranteed, your bookcases, tablets, and book devices will be overflowing. Wasn't it frustrating, when on vacation, you couldn't finish a paperback and then picked it up on your next trip and forgot everything you read? Never again in retirement.

Now you can write and enjoy it.

You can learn old school cursive again, a lost art. It's coming back now. Maybe the new normal. There are even coloring book workshops and quill pen writing sessions all over the world to get the brain working. Writing clearly has become a lost art with the E- or I-everything age. Be careful and be patient as it will take time recognizing your own handwriting again. Don't worry, it eventually all comes together with practice. I speak from experience.

You no longer need to feel guilt anymore.

You have experienced everything you could feel guilty about already, and then some. Mentally thriving retirees, re-toolingees, or re-inventees, whichever you prefer, seem to have an inner peace which possibly could be a result of no more guilt thoughts. Notice that the successful ones automatically do righteous things versus guilt-ridden things. It could be a "stairway to heaven" phenomenon — as they get closer to the inevitable.

If you are writing books and articles and consulting, based on your work wisdom, you're thriving mentally in retirement.

Also, if you mastered some computer skills, but still need the Geek Squad and kids as a resource on occasion, then you're doing well. The Geek Squad is another great way to hire out work to free up your time. And they are better and more cooperative than your IT department was at work, right? Writing and consulting is a no-brainer. You don't need to do any research nor do any prep time. Your vast experience and knowledge from work is enough to be successful. Don't be embarrassed by the high fees you can collect — you are worth it.

If you are really tired of or don't understand the workings of iPhones, smartphones, tablets, etc., then dump them.

Get a common cell phone with big numbers on it. If you have to learn computer gadget skills, then learn from your grandkids — they won't charge you much. Here's an idea. If you're a cook, get a smart pan. It transmits temperature data via an app and lets you know when it's time for the next recipe step. Come on, really? Einstein said it best, "I fear the day when technology will surpass our human interaction — the world will have a generation of idiots." A generation? We have several non-communicative generations of idiots. Even old people are selling out.

For your mental well-being, live life in projects.

Your retirement life can be a series of projects. Life itself can be a project broken down into such things as: coaching your spouse and kids, playing with your grandkids, managing your property, handling your finances, writing articles, shopping, doing odd jobs around the house, and even cooking. No new skills are needed and living life this way keeps your mind active.

*Enjoy living without hierarchy.
You are "it" now.*

As the hierarchy your new normal is lobbying for senior citizen rights. Like two days per week, ten percent off on groceries instead of one day. And a ten percent discount on wine and beer purchases every day. But don't lobby in the context of protest marches like in the 60s and 70s. You don't need to re-live your youth in this manner. It's not good for your older/wiser image and reputation, plus being "hierarchy" in jail is not cool.

Never take anything too seriously.

Laughter is the best medicine and it activates the dopamine and endorphins very well — medical practitioners say it's been clinically proven. They also say that serious people lose their will to live. In the "2000-Year-Old Man" series, Mel Brooks is asked how he lived to be so old. He stated, "The will to live — Dr. William Talive — a great man." What several people have noticed about retirees is that they seem to have recovered or discovered a very hilarious sense of humor — a good thing to help make the world a happier place.

*If alone and feeling uncomfortable,
then try noise.*

The stereo, CNN, BBC, old movies, and reality TV work very well. And going out with people who you really enjoy being with can be very exhilarating. You might find yourself showing up early to outings, parties, meetings, etc., because you're so excited to go out. I recently showed up a whole month early, but punctual regarding the correct hour, for a meeting with our World Vision volunteer group — a little embarrassing.

*It's really OK not to know what day it is.
But don't go comatose.*

Shortly after retirement a colleague had this thought, "Stop and smell the roses, but don't stay in the garden too long." The mind could turn to mush and you might lose track of days, weeks, and even months — not good. The thriving retirees often don't know what day it is because there are no more days off, vacations, nor weekends. Every day is either a day off or a day on — no distinction of off and on anymore. Isn't this great?

Don't read serious self-help books, like "How to" do yoga, be happy, be fit, be positive, meditate, etc.

Question: Did you read a manual on how to ride a bike? No. You DO yoga and meditation with an instructor. You ARE happy, fit, and positive because you choose to be. Presuming your work-life was a success, you probably are the best you can be right now. If people are still giving you these books, then use the old cliché, "You can't teach an old dog new tricks," which is a good way to say no.

Dig into your skills and experiences toolbox daily.

Use it to live. Note: see The Mantra section toward the end of the book. Some tools include: eat well, sleep well, exercise. Or C.O.P.E: confidence, optimism, positive attitude, and enthusiasm. My father-in-law, whom this book is dedicated to, retired from the car industry and built two very large houses, renovated another one, and refurbished several classic cars and a motorcycle, in Asia, in a timespan of just four years. His DNA for success was confidence and a very positive attitude. He C.O.P.E.'d very well doing a lot of things he didn't or couldn't do before.

Don't grow old gracefully.

Grow old loudly, with passion, and a little reckless abandon. Gals, go to high school boys' volleyball and basketball games. Guys, go to girls' volleyball and basketball games. My 93-year-old father and his 96-year-old buddy go regularly. They are the teams' best and loudest fans. Regarding reckless abandon these two guys have been quoted as saying, "If I'd known that I would live so long, I would have taken better care of myself." They have lived the secret sauce of surreal retirement for a long time.

Fear, guilt, and worry are no longer in your mental DNA.

Retirees, particularly in their way-past-80s, do remarkable things. There was no fear, guilt, nor worry when my grandfather, with his helper, visited the Holy Lands well into his 80s. What's interesting in life is that young kids and old people seem to not have these negative mental traits. There is a human spirit about them that leads to a carefree life. It's only life in between where fear, guilt, and worry is a problem. We can all learn from this.

EMOTIONAL

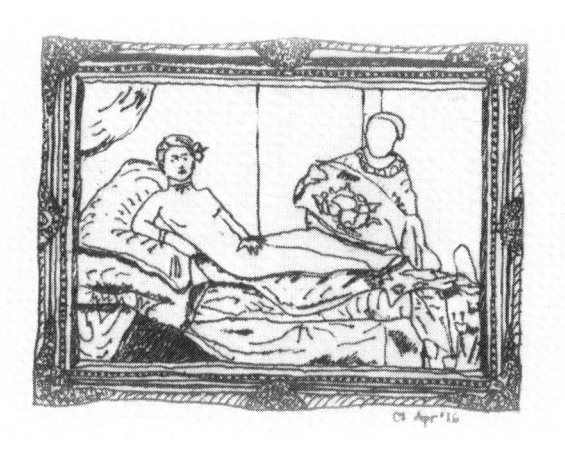

Being retired, you will notice paintings and photography on all the walls and the artifacts in the rooms for maybe the first time. Enjoy and keep asking yourself, "Where did that come from?"

Get into a relaxed state, be silent, and see the world that you never saw before. For some reason the museums you used to frequent seem a whole lot different. "Gee, I didn't notice that T. rex before! And where did that P-51 Mustang on the ceiling come from?" Note that both have always been there at two museums in Chicago. One guesses that the "Spirit of St. Louis" might now be present for you at the Smithsonian Air & Space Museum. During our working life very few wonderful things were noticed — blame it on distractions.

If you are alone (not lonely, heaven forbid) during the day, then enjoy it.

When your spouse comes home from work, you will talk a lot and get excited like a dog who hasn't seen its master in a hundred years. Your spouse hears about fifty percent of what you say — not bad, life is good — that's thriving in retirement. Weekends can be tough on your spouse during your excitement. They can't wait for Monday morning. Also, you will stay in touch with your kids a lot more. You will be the mom or dad they never saw very much.

Be charming.
There is no reason to be ruthless anymore.

There is a sort of light-headedness and grace in successful retirees. It catches acquaintances off guard if they remember their emotions during the working days. A Scottish plant manager lived his working life being ruthlessly compassionate and compassionately ruthless. Not a bad oxymoronic combination in the work environment when you get used to it. He was wonderful to work with, but drove his wife, kids, and out-of-office friends nuts. Realizing this, he retired, changed his hard-driving ways, re-invented himself, and has been quite pleasant and charming ever since.

*Don't laugh at yourself anymore.
You can now laugh at others —
you've earned the rite of passage.*

Based on your vast experiences, you will now see others do very stupid things — causing them to laugh at themselves. Touché. Remember young-acting Biff laughing at himself as the mature, successfully retired Marty McFly was commanding him to wash his car correctly in one of the "Back to the Future" movies? Smile all the time. If you can't, then grin a lot. There is scientific proof that you use less energy and muscles smiling than frowning. As we get older we need to conserve these things.

Never stop appreciating beautiful, passionate, and emotional people.

This means your spouse, family, and friends. They might be people you have known for years (rekindle the relationship wisely) and/or new people you want to be with who bring you back to the emotions of youth. Younger people, companions and friends, can help rejuvenate you with new places, new mobility, and a passionate life to experience again. Case in point, Demi Moore married Ashton Kutcher. And life is too short to be with negative people. Been there done that — not fun.

Your main goal in life should be to be as humorous as possible.

But try to remember not to tell the same jokes over and over again — the ones you have known all your life. My father's friends ask me the same question all the time, "Have you heard this one before?" You reply, "Oh, yes, several times." Three guys in their 90s, including my dad, went out to dinner whereby two very good-looking, well-endowed women chatted them up. Their picture was taken and it ended up on social media with the caption: "A good pair beats three of a kind." Humor in retirement.

You never have to say you're sorry anymore.

"Love means never having to say you're sorry." Circa 1970s, the "Love Story" movie — come on. Retirement, circa now. Instead of "I'm sorry," it's "Hey, I'm 63 you're 40 or 30 or 20-something. Get over it." People will expect you to slip up, do or say something stupid every once in a while. Your family and friends will watch you like a hawk for the least hint of losing it and expect some sort of apology. You counter with, "Hey, I'm old school, what do I know about the crazy world of today. Sorry, for what?" To be a little bit provocative, "Please get over it and I'll try not to do it again," is the new, "I'm sorry."

Live life with no regrets.

Joe Pesci, in the movie "With Honors," used this as his mantra. He died a happy man living life to the fullest with his Harvard college buddies. Many business people regret not working full-out anymore in retirement, and regret retiring — period. The result can be fatal with nothing to live for anymore, they can't adjust to retirement, and there's nothing on the horizon. Fill the void and get rid of the regret; build schools, teach, sing in the choir, sponsor Junior Rotarians, play cards, join book clubs, etc.

As a senior citizen, you don't need to take any more schtick (a.k.a. crap).

Like from taxi drivers, airline check-in clerks, pool attendants, receptionists, doctors, bankers, lawyers, etc. Remember, you are the hierarchy, you are the elder. All of these people are younger than you and less experienced, right? Be assertive. If you fall into the normal subservient role, get energized. Men, watch "Grumpy Old Men." Women, watch "Golden Girls." Retirement research has provided the following story. An over 70s guy in Florida was caught peeing in the pool by a pool attendant. The pool attendant shouted, "No!" so loud that the gentleman fell into the pool. Go figure.

When alone get to know store owners, coffee shop clerks, and restaurant and bar staff.

I'm sure everyone working has wondered why our retired moms and dads like talking to these people and even strangers on the street. Now, as retirees, we know. It's fun. We discover some very interesting people after our work years. So, if the store or restaurant is closed, improvise — go back to the TV, read, call your friends/kids/etc., listen to music, do yoga, meditate, pray, or else drive your spouse crazy.

*Getting angry takes years off your life
and you don't have that much time left.
Two thirds of your life is already lived.*

Don't panic, having one third left is pretty good. Use the time wisely. We see angry retirees and don't understand why they still yell at the political system, bash the President, have contempt with Congress, the Democrats, and Republicans. And then there is the bashing of the new generations. Let them be. They should get over it. In retirement accept what is and enjoy your life. Otherwise you will end up at the home, aka, the Zombie Hotel. This is where you can check out any time you like, but you can never leave.

ද

Since you no longer have a caring boss, care for yourself.

Take time for yourself. But don't be selfish. Charity work is extremely satisfying and brings on the emotional endorphins. And it's not like "giving back." This is an erroneous term. I'm sure you've worked hard, helped others, contributed to society. There is no need to "give back." Your previous life was not handed to you on a silver platter — you worked for it and gave a lot. Achieving a balance of taking care of yourself and taking care of others is a great thing — an emotional rescue.

Pet and talk to your cat and/or dog daily.

Yes, have conversations with them, particularly when you are alone. Hey, do it even when people are around — everybody does. There is no reason for concern that you're going nuts. In retirement you will notice these dog/cat talks become much richer. And you think that they think you're wonderful and understand you completely. You say, "No, Whiteshoes, you can't eat Sandy's food." Actually she probably hears, "Blah, blah, blah." But you don't know that and she seems to understand what you said not to do anyway — phenomenal. Here's a thought: PETA should give all shelter animals to retirees. This is a win-win-win for PETA, the retiree, and the animal.

Be content — no needs, no wants.

This is a great definition of contentment that I received from a very wise Japanese woman who ran one of the largest retail chains in Asia. All our working lives we strive for more and more of everything — wealth, happiness, health, wisdom, and possessions. It's time to take a break, and retirement is a perfect opportunity. As mentioned we no longer need new clothes — the old ones will outlive us anyway. Nor do we need to party as much as we used to, get a new physique, new skills, or learn something new. Total inner peace is accepting people and the world around us as it is. This is the key to emotional fulfillment in retirement.

*Get some of your teenage personality back.
Be a seenager (senior teenager).*

A mid-70-year-old stated, "I have everything that I wanted as a teenager, only 60 years later. But I don't have acne, and people I hang around with aren't scared of getting pregnant." It's OK to act like a kid every once in a while and feel young. To support this guys, get some Paco Rabanne or English Leather cologne. Gals, get some Chanel No 5 or Opium perfume — relive the '70s. Recently I didn't recognize a previous partner of mine who reinvented herself physically and emotionally. She looked and acted like she did back in 1975. She was thriving, like in her younger years, but now in retirement.

Lighten up and chill out.

Laugh out loud, do something different. Those who are good at this make 180-degree career moves in retirement and become very successful. Chefs become TV stars like Anthony Bourdain and Bobby Chin; doctors, and rock stars like Bono, do charity work with the Gates Foundation; the football star, Eddie George, retooled and became a successful Broadway star; nurses have become caregivers. These people and many others have lightened up, chilled out, and are having the time of their lives. Work, definitely, isn't a four-letter word.

Don't fear police, doctors, or dentists anymore.

When you were young, not so long ago, they were all older than you — representing the "respect your elders" adage and often coming across very intimidating. Now that you're the elder, acknowledge them, but don't revere them anymore. You have to smile when a young, wet-behind-the-ears, inexperienced policeman pulls you over for speeding. He sees your stash of firearms in the backseat and asks, "Sir, what are you afraid of?" You reply, "Not a damn thing, sonny boy!"

FAMILY AND FRIENDS

If you retire and have property in exciting and beautiful places, you will seldom have to visit anyone.

They will visit you. It is your property, you worked for it, your terra firma, and your permanent domicile; that which you now have that you didn't have when you moved all over the place for work. And you are likely to see your kids, grandkids, and friends a lot more in an exciting beautiful place.

You have the time to rekindle old friendships. But be patient — they might need time to adjust to seeing you again.

The same 75-year-old gentleman who eats pie, ice cream, and cake for lunch stated, "Be mindful that happiness isn't based on possessions, power, or prestige, but on relationships with people we like, respect, and enjoy spending time with." Some retirees call it networking, a term they just can't forget from the working days. High school and college reunions take on a whole new meaning — they are quite fun now, although attendance is dwindling, which is a natural attrition.

*You've been taking care of others for so long —
now it's time for others to take care of you.*

In some parts of the world like Asia and South America, kids are arranging for their retired parents to move in with them. This is a whole new dynamic for both generations to cope with. If you've been raised in a type "A" personality family, it is not recommended to do this. It would be a chaotic, s**tstorm-ish environment. The retired parents, however, would get the most out of this deal because they'd have the kids to take care of them.

For a great day out with the grandkids, visit the recycle can-eater at the grocery store.

Or take them to the dump to unload all the old junk you don't want — preferable in the vehicle of choice — an old pickup truck. Oh and make sure you are called something respectful like Pops, Mimi, PopPop, Mimes, or Mimaw. Grandma and Grandpa are too old school these days. You don't need to go to movie theatres anymore. Watch Disney, Pixar, or DreamWorks DVDs with the little ones. Also, you have once more earned the right of passage to cry watching these films. Tell the kids about the time when you were their age and cried when Ol' Yeller died.

With everyone thinking you have lots of spare time, they might expect you to take care of everybody and everything.

This could include personal counseling, domestic chores, errands, trip planning, finances, cleaning, cooking, emotional rescue, and so forth. Do it in moderation. If you don't "be conservative" with all this, then it will become an obsession like work was. However, it is great for your emotional bank account that your spouse is holding on you. And it's an easy skill set to pick up — no need for a self-help book on this stuff.

Outlive your spouse — he/she needs you.

You will be their coach, mentor, sponsor, companion, and best friend. Be with them now that you have the time. Again, just think of the huge balance you are creating in your emotional bank account with him or her. You will be able to get out of going to functions or outings you really don't want to go to and he/she will forgive you. You can also leave clothes lying around and watch TV he or she doesn't like. But remember to keep topping the account with quality time spent together.

Your kids will tell you it's OK to talk trash every once in a while.

You get a pass, you're old. A lot of us have a story about being with our older retired parents while driving in the car and mom turns to dad and says something like, "Honey you were supposed to take a frickin' right back there." Dad replies, "Honey I know what I'm doing, shut your damn cake hole." Blame it on getting old. "Dateline BBC" internet news, April 4th, 2016: "A study has shown that swearing relieves stress, depression, and burnout." Go figure — life is good. Balance the sometimes rude behavior with a little gentleness. Like sending your kids pictures of you petting the dog looking gay-ish, or posing in your favorite Wallace and Gromit t-shirt or FCUK fashion designer shirt (French Connection UK — I know what you were thinking).

ε

Play with your kids again and your grandkids. You now have time.

Family becomes more important, as they should. Now is the time to get to know them better without being obnoxious and overstaying your welcome at their place. You were probably away a lot while working, so rekindle family friendships. Before passing away Steve Jobs said, "Treasure the love for your family, spouse and friends. Cherish yourself and others." This "time" thing is interesting. At work you had discretionary (chill out) time, and non-discretionary (work) time. Some of us never really understood those terms, especially as it related to work files management. Now we do — it's all discretionary time in retirement. You're in charge.

And ... babysit your younger friends' kids. They keep you young and remind you to not have any more.

For men, a little goes a long way. Quality time is OK, not quantity. Women tend to go overboard on not only time spent with their grandkids, but their friends' kids as well. Some want to take care of them all the time. It might have something to do with wanting to be a full-time mom again. As if this role wasn't enough in the younger years. I haven't come across many retired men who want to become dads again.

Take care of your spouse so he/she won't drive you, the kids, and grandkids crazy.

Another good reason to outlive him/her. Working spouses can be a handful with stress and burnout. When the kids and grandkids visit it can be a real s**t-storm. You have the time so you can devote hours in the evening for calming them down, and talking through the issues, often without much sleep. The back rubs and massages you've learned to master help your spouse sleep, much to the dismay of your own plight. But you can adjust because now you can justifiably sleep in way past 9 a.m.

If you're fortunate to still have your mom and/ or dad around, then see them, be with them, drive them to church.

This too in moderation. Growing up with parents for so long was OK, but you're not in Kansas anymore. The fun part is when they (and you) confess certain things that happened in the past, and both parties are completely unaware as to how things really went down. "Son, remember when I told you XYZ? Well what really happened is ABC." Or, "Dad, remember when I did DEF? Well, I really did HIJ." It was so long ago that both parties are now forgiven.

You will be like a godfather or godmother for your family — your spouse, sisters, brothers, kids, grandkids.

Your retirement stability and bliss will be like a rock for them as you age. They need you and you need them. On the lighter side of life here's a good one: Following a physical with his doctor, and with good results, a 70-year-old gentleman asked if he would make it to 80. His doctor asked, "Do you smoke, drink, take drugs, eat red meat, spend a lot of time in the sun, gamble, or drive fast cars?" The man replied, "No, I don't do any of those things." The doctor retorted, "Then why do you even give a damn if you want to live to 80?!"

Never have your grown-up kids nor grandkids stay with you longer than a week.

It's wonderful to enjoy your grandkids and when you've had enough, which you will if you're a guy, you can give them back to your kids. Something you couldn't do with your own children. And when the stress and noise levels get too high, your son or daughter will instruct you to go up to your man-cave to chill. This is enjoying family and friends while thriving in retirement.

SPIRITUAL

Ahhh retirement.
In the words of the band "Yes," "Just what keeps us alive, just what makes us survive —
our home is our world, our life."

Where your heart is, there your home is also. (Apologies for the cliché.) There is a phenomenon in the world today. People do live longer in certain parts of the world. The highest number of 100-plus-year-olds live in Senegal, West Africa and Okinawa, Japan. Go figure. Oh, gosh, let's go move there — not. Other notable locations include Arizona, Florida, Hunan, China, Thailand, and even northwest Michigan. What is it? The water? Food? Scenery? Lifestyle? Zen-ness? Maybe all of these things. My father still wears his 30-year-old sweatshirt (he doesn't buy new clothes either) which says, "If Heaven isn't like northwest Michigan, then I'm not going."

Make peace with God.

You will be in heaven sooner than you'd probably like to be. Why has it been noted that there is a "Highway to Hell" and a "Stairway to Heaven"? If it's based on the amount of traffic and the speed in which we arrive, we are in trouble. The two rock bands who wrote those songs should have collaborated on this a bit. We all trust they got it backwards. Don't you think? Anyway, after your working years the quiet time is wonderful for prayer. We can pray often and with more concentration and resolve than we had before.

*If you live close to a beach, then walk it.
If you live in the mountains, then hike them. If you live near a lake, then swim it.
All spiritually uplifting.*

Reflecting on this an Australian Levi Strauss retiree summed it up, "The most significant occurrence and awareness for me is I have become wiser, more tolerant, a better listener, and more worldly since retiring. I believe the reason for this is I have ceased to become insular in my observation of the beautiful world around me. Existing in a surreal world is living your dreams which, we could not do during our working lives." He now lives on a beach in Southeast Asia.

The coolest thing about retiring in the mountains is seeing a reverse, double sunset.

There are orange, red, and purple colors to the east lighting up the clouds, and then the real sunset is behind the mountains to the west — it's like a double fantasy cheap thrill — very spiritual. So get your favorite beverage, pull up a chair, get into a meditative state, and experience the awesomeness. Our Asian family and friends go nuts for this view while visiting us in the hills of Phuket, Thailand.

Listen and don't talk too much.
People will think you're really wise.

Be a responsible wise person; take retirement and your twilight years seriously because young people need to learn from you and revere you. Don't let them down. Also, listen to what they have to say, ask questions and help them in their journey through life. This isn't easy given that it's the norm for the younger generations to be talking incoherently all the time, fidgeting, and being impatient with an attention span of about eight seconds. Aristotle gave us a good tip: "We would be better and braver to inquire [ask questions] than to indulge in the idle fancy that we already know [everything]."

Be wise, tell stories.

Wise people have more material than younger generations. It's often called: "The Yoda Syndrome of Old People." Just don't use his voice. Sometimes the old and wise people mumble, often for effect, and we can't understand them, but they do have more history than us. The mumbling could be to mimic the aforementioned issue of the internet generations who have lost the skill of speaking articulately.

*Never raise your voice except
in jubilation and praise.*

If you have had the privilege of hearing Billy Graham live in a packed stadium you will experience loud jubilation and praise — it is wonderful. I was blessed in 1985 to hear Graham speak to 100,000 people at the Sunderland, England soccer stadium — my ears are still ringing. As a side note, some of us have a hard time raising our voice because our lung capacity is less than it used to be. Others are loud constantly due to hearing loss. Maybe that was Billy's secret. But I don't believe so. He was the most jubilant and all-praising person I've ever seen.

*Meditate and reflect daily,
even if you don't know how to.*

It's OK to fake it. Yoga is good too. But know your limits. For the first practice it is advised to not learn yoga in India from a well-seasoned yoga master. I had a session in Goa, India whereby I was nearly put in traction as a result of severe back, knee, arm, and neck pain. Convalescing took over a week and walking was difficult. I now stick to meditation. Reflection is good. Spend fifteen minutes each day letting thoughts, emotions, and feelings go in one side of the brain and out the other.

Be philosophical every once in a while, maybe even a little bit pompous and bold.

You have earned the right. You can speak analogies (albeit clichés) like: 1) The grass is always greener on the other side. 2) Stop and smell the roses, but don't stay in the garden too long. 3) Close the book on work, but remember the chapters. But don't be obnoxious about it. The pompousness and boldness I'm advocating is best described with a story. At a new seniors' complex, the manager stated the rules such as: "The female sleeping quarters are out-of-bounds for males, and the male dormitory is off limits to the females. Anybody caught breaking the rule the first time will be fined $20, $60 for the second time, and $180 the third time. Are there any questions?" "Yes," said an older woman, "How much for a season pass?"

Build schools for less-fortunate kids.

These children are fun to be with, they appreciate you, the teachers and government officials need you, and it keeps you active. Starting in 2003 retirees and actives from primarily large MNC's in Asia, Europe, and America formed the Executives for the Extraordinary (E4E) in partnership with the World Vision Foundation of Thailand to build one school per year in Greater Asia. To date, our team of between 18 to 25 participants have built 13 schools across the Asian region. The year end project completion during Thanksgiving week, brings the school kids and teachers, country/government officials, E4E, and World Vision together to finish the school. This is our boot camp: concrete work, painting, landscaping, finishing the construction work, and the best part, teaching English to the kids, singing songs, and playing sports with them. We turn the school over to the community, government, teachers and kids on the last day via a huge ceremony.

Discover the way to make this world a better place.

As a retiree the possibility to make a difference, to create the kingdom of Heaven on earth (a school or community housing project, infrastructure, agriculture, or healthcare programs and projects) is limitless all over the world. Think about it. NGO's are everywhere: World Vision, Red Cross, Habitat for Humanity, Vista, Peace Corp, the One project, the Gates Foundation, and notably, to end poverty in our lifetime, the UN Millennium project.

You don't necessarily need to respect your elders anymore — you are one.

My father puts it this way, "I was raised to respect my elders, but now I can't find any!" Take heed and do not revert to, "I'm your elder, respect me." The notion of earning it still applies universally. Also, have you noticed that all 60s, 70s, 80s, and 90s folks seem to band together, almost communally, where the age difference no longer matters and the old rules don't apply. It's so enlightening seeing retired 60-year-olds hanging out and bonding with 90-year-olds. There seems to be respected friendships popping up across all of these age groups — spiritually thriving in retirement.

Understand the distinction: being alone versus lonely.

Being alone is good — it can be very spiritual. Being lonely means you are doing nothing and are bored, or not thriving in retirement. Remember, you were with hundreds of people when you were working so give yourself a break. Talk to yourself (or to your dog). It's OK, don't be embarrassed, no one is around. You can sing, dance, play air guitar, plan your projects, meditate, do yoga, and anything else that requires only one participant— like watching reality TV court trials or managing your property and finances. An alone gentleman wanted a companion so he went to see a man who was selling his talking dog for $10. He asked the dog what his story was. The dog said he worked for the CIA gathering intelligence during meetings between world powers, learned trade secrets from China, and informed the UN on plans for nuclear armament in North Korea, via closed-door sessions that he attended. The gentleman asked the owner why the talking dog was so cheap. The owner replied, "Because he's a damn liar."

Pray constantly.

You've made it this far in life — God has put His trust and faith in you, now trust and have faith in Him. When my dad isn't at the high school girls' volleyball and basketball games, or hanging out at his favorite watering hole with his 96-year-old buddy, he states on our weekly Skype sessions, "I'm not lonely, just alone and I talk a lot to our Maker — I'm content, no needs, nor wants. It's all good." 'Sixties and 70s retirees can learn from the 80s and 90s folks. They don't worry about all the things that they thought would do them in like weight gain, favorite beverage, the occasional cigar or Virginia Slims, active lifestyle, diverse diet, etc. They are very positive people, understand moderation, are determined to live life to the fullest, and believe in the power of prayer.

Strive for excellence versus perfection. Sometimes good enough is OK.

The frustrated perfectionists leave their company, want to semi-retire and work for a similar company performing their same skill set, and strive for that perfection they felt they did not achieve in their previous endeavor. Why? The successful semi-retirees do the 180-degree career shift mentioned before, find satisfaction being good, great, and even excellent in new endeavors. The evidence shows in people like Lamar Johnson, P&G Market Development Executive to University of Texas Executive Director; President Carter to Habitat for Humanity; a brain surgeon friend of mine to botanist; Ted Nugent, a rock legend to political activist; and, as mentioned before, one of the best running backs of all-time, Eddie George, is now acting on Broadway. Maybe breaking the perfectionist syndrome means reinventing yourself in retirement; and now for something completely different.

FINANCIAL

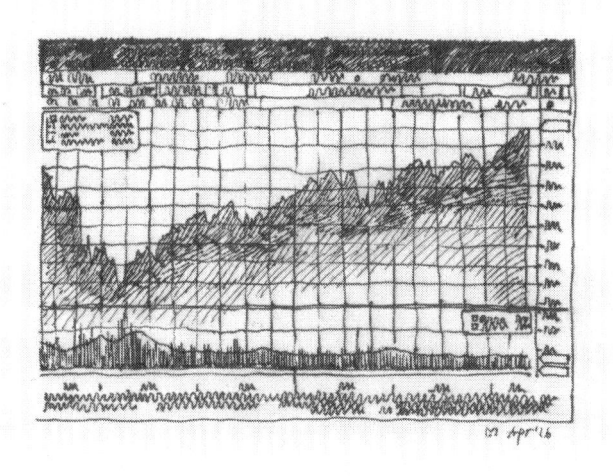

Donate your dress clothes, fancy shoes, good socks, and stockings to a worthy charity or relatives.

Keep only what you need for church, weddings, and funerals. And remember, the clothes you cherish and love, like worn-out jeans and moccasins, will outlast you — no need to buy new. Donating also eliminates the need for your kids to have to throw them out or give them away when you "go."

You probably were successful and famous in business. Be successful and famous in retirement – flaunt it.

Start an LLC (Limited Liability Company). You can write-off your expenses for charity trips and whatever work you do, show income from book sales, consulting, tutoring, gifts from clients, etc. It's better for your LLC to be sued versus you personally if you screw something up, right?

Spend the kids' inheritance — or at least try to.

Take homage of the very old cliché (sorry, I can't help it): "You can't take it with you when you go." This might sound barbaric, but your financial advisor will urge you to make sure there is money left for your kids and that you should curb your spending. Why? Because they make more money on your account when it's more full. Another of dad's 30-year-old sweatshirts says, "I'm (definitely) spending my kid's inheritance." He's not feeling the guilt his advisor puts on him. And another thing: Are you tired of hearing your parents complain that they are now on a fixed income and you have to pay for dinners and such? There is no such thing as a fixed income during retirement. Take out as much as you want and need from savings, pension, stocks, etc. Not many thriving retirees just live off their fixed social security income.

Own or rent two properties — one for summer and one for winter — it's the worldly way. A universal rite of passage for successful retirees.

Just be nice to the locals so they won't rip off your stuff. And make sure you have the right clothes to match the climate in each location — a mistake we all make. Who needs sweaters in Thailand or a speedo in northern Michigan — duh. Owning a tropical paradise can be bliss. But, as mentioned, only if you have someone else to take care of it. If you've invested in nice places, then you don't have to stay in hotels anymore. Plan ahead on where you want to live — don't leave it to the last minute. A UK friend of mine in Singapore just retired. I asked him where he was going to spend his summers and winters. His reply went something like this, "I really don't know if I want to live in South Africa, Asia, the UK, or the U.S.A." What?

*Give and donate your time and money —
it's all you have.*

And remember this is not "giving back," it's helping those you love and those in need. When you're a little strapped for cash, donate your time to a worthy cause. When you win the lottery, donate your cash. On one of our World Vision school projects, in a dire straits part of Indonesia, after an exhaustive week working in poor weather and squalor conditions, the WV staff brought us t-shirts which made our day. The shirts read, "One Life, Do Something."

*Investigate a reverse mortgage —
take the collateral and enjoy it.*

The jury is still out on this piece of advice, but might be worth checking out. The point is if you want to live in the manner you have been accustomed to, look at ways to increase your cash reserves. We are all inundated with advice pre and post retirement. Be wary of the retirement periodicals. One such firm sends out a 150-page, tiny print report on how to handle your wealth upon retirement — tips, financial tools, analysis, graphs, charts, case studies, "what-if's," upside/downside, issues, havens, fund information, law firm suggestions like Dewey, Cheatem, and Howe, etc.. If we want to thrive in retirement, we don't have time for this how-to advice. Hire it out to a sound financial advisor.

Make sure your banker and financial advisor are your best friends.

But as mentioned, don't take any schtick from them, and don't believe everything they tell you. Often financial advisors farm out the back-office asset management to big financial firms. The problem comes when these companies do an analysis on your wealth, suggest cutting expenses, being less risky, and reporting worse case scenarios for money draining and market conditions. They can cause panic. No kidding? Relax, your best friend advisor will set the record straight, calm you down, and give you confidence that all is well; don't do anything differently. You're financially all right.

Pay attention to the stock market, daily. It's probably how you're getting paid.

Fixed income like Social Security isn't enough if you want to live life large. The ante on market performance is "up-ed" significantly during retirement. Remember when you were working, the markets would tank, and the comment was, "Oh, it's only a paper loss, it will come back, no worries." Now — you're not in Kansas anymore — it's a real loss. Another flaw in reading the retirement periodicals is that often the author recommends stock investments like: "Now is the time to invest in retailer XYZ, a great buy." After doing some investigation it turns out the author is already heavily invested in this company, is losing money, and the retailer is in trouble. Your bank and/or your financial advisors are your most qualified resources of choice.

*Do your net worth statement
in your head, monthly.*

This will ensure your money outlasts you. And never balance your checkbook ever again. It takes up too much of your precious time and everything will work out financially in the end. I hate to beat a dead horse, but here's the last outrageous tip from one of the retirement periodicals. It reads: "Make sure when your family, including your kids, are all gathered together for the holidays, let's say Thanksgiving for example, that you outline what should happen when you die in terms of funeral arrangements, wealth disbursement, and property management." Gee, that sounds like a great holiday experience — like a you-know-what in the punchbowl. Can you imagine how screwed up and depressing that holiday would be?

If all goes well financially, you don't have to be a greeter at Walmart nor a street vendor in big cities.

But as noted before, at least you don't need any new skills for either of these noble endeavors. What's interesting is that in developing countries like Southeast Asia, you will never see any old people working in grocery, retail stores, or street kiosks. The culture dictates that the children will take care of their parents the rest of their lives. How cool is that. And, as an added bonus, the children will move them into their house. A Chinese couple I know sometimes keep in touch to find out when I'm out at our favorite watering hole; then they can take a break from ma and pa and join me.

Never painstakingly comparative-shop anymore. Just buy — there's not much time left.

Men really get this. The shortest distance between outside the store and what you need is a straight line. We stay on task — no browsing, no buying on impulse, no buying stuff just because it's on sale, no comparing prices, and no going down all aisles and in all mall shops in case you missed something. In Asia and South America, women shop long hours, daily. To meet this demand, in most Asian big cities, each office tower building has a mall underneath. Well, there goes the productivity.

Enjoy watching everyone else work and/or talk about work.

It's one of the great retirement past times, as you mumble to yourself, "Boy am I glad to be free of that. Been there, done that, got the ulcer." One doesn't need to work all their life. We reach our level of ineffectiveness faster than we think. Like when a retired engineer decides to get his or her real estate license, tries to do this into their twilight years, and gets lost trying to find the property they handle in order to show a client. Also, be patient when you're with working colleagues who describe all or most of the issues you went through, like employee relations or lack thereof, production issues, irate customers, complaints of R&D not working well with the manufacturing plants, sales clerk attrition issues, not enough staff, not enough budget money, missed sales forecasts, etc. Coach them, help them, and be empathetic with them. They will appreciate it.

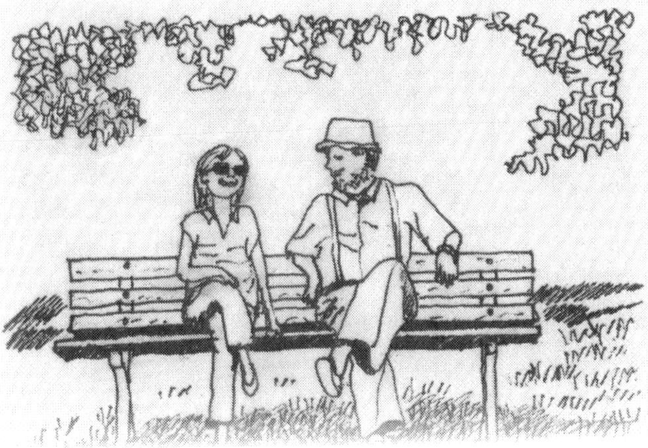

INTERVIEWS WITH THE OVER 60S FOLKS

What follows are interviews with a very diverse set of successful retirees from all over the world, some fresh to the new life and some very seasoned to retirement. The context of these interviews address the retirees thoughts, feelings, and experiences with the eight DNA elements of retirement life. Their responses are rich, enlightening, and insightful. I've quoted them often in the book as they fully support the eight element perspectives, stories, and experiences gleaned from a vast group of colleagues who've given great input. I trust you will feel the same and believe that this section rounds out the premise that retirement can be both surreal and exciting — and that the possibility of the best days of your life and a wonderful adventure is ahead.

Somphan Eamrungroj — Senior Executive Vice President, The Export-Import Bank of Thailand. Retired September 30, 2013.

1. Regarding your way of being, how would you like this element to be in retirement?

As we age through our lives, I personally believe that we, mortals, adapt to the changes both from the inside and outside. Therefore, it is not just at retirement time and beyond that we have this mentioned element, but it is with us since we were born.

2. What lifestyle changes would you like to make during retirement?

During retirement I certainly think that my lifestyle would be subject to my physical and mental states at future moments in time. In such context, lifestyle adaptations are essential to enable me in living in harmony with the social, natural, and economic environments.

3. From a physical perspective what changes would you like to make?

I would like to eat less, have just adequate rest, and walk more often in the parks.

4. Mentally speaking what are your thoughts about how sound you would like your mind to be?

I believe we have grown to retirement age through successes and failures. I have learned valuable lessons both from life experiences and from good books. I have been a watcher of people around me seeing them grow or dwindle, laugh or cry, etc. As a watcher of people I reflectively watch myself from time to time. Such exercises keep me in balance.

5. What emotional changes would you like to make after leaving the workforce?

Detachment from the people who surrounded me when I was working is the most crucial, but difficult thing to do after retirement. It took a while to achieve detachment. Just like a wave washing ashore, I am not different. I simply fade away.

6. Spiritually speaking please share your insights on changes and/or enhancements you would like to make in retirement.

I revisit places where I had fond memories. I listen to songs and music that once made me happy. Walking in the park is currently my most favorite pastime as it keeps me physically well at the same time that I enjoy the company of other retirees walking similarly in the park.

7. What goals do you have regarding financial stability?

My financial goal is to match my future needs against the financial resources saved over the years at the grind.

Chomsuda Tuntariyanond — Executive Vice President, The Export-Import Bank of Thailand. Retired September 30, 2015.

After having worked for 40 years in the banking business (treasury department), a little rest is what I was looking forward to. I have had so many good experiences and have learned a lot from my job and my good colleagues, but the time has come for me to spend more time on myself and family.

On Way of Being and Lifestyle:

My pace of life has changed a bit, I am more relaxed and enjoy life more, more time for my parents (now only my mother), my husband and my five dogs.

I was lucky to have been able to spend more time with my Dad a month before he passed away. As for Mom who is now 88 years old, she still goes to work every day at the school in the palace (Chitralada School) where she used to teach. She never wants to retire and stay at home. Therefore, I will visit her once or twice a week.

On Physical, Mental, Emotional and Spiritual:

Healthwise, I am much better, I exercise more (I used to be an active sportsperson playing tennis, badminton, and golf, but stopped completely since my Dad had a stroke). My blood pressure is back to normal; cholesterol, triglyceride etc. are under control, unlike before retirement. I guess I did not realize that my body was under stress from work because I did not feel bad and was enjoying every day of work. For your information I still have regular contacts with friends and colleagues at the bank.

As for my mind, emotional-wise, I have always been quite sound, happy going. I did not have to adjust much after retirement.

As for financial stability, I and my husband have planned savings long before we actually retired, therefore, I do not feel the financial stress from my retirement

As for whether there is anything that I would like to change regarding being with family and friends during retirement, my answer is that there is nothing I could think of at present. Everything has been, and is, good with them.

In conclusion, I am thoroughly enjoying my life after retirement!

Dr. Robert L. Willard — M.D. Ophthalmology, Toledo, Ohio. Retired September, 1989.

1. Way of Being. I went through quite an adjustment. Particularly moving from metro Toledo to the middle of nowhere in northern Michigan. It took many months to not wake up at 6 am every day,which drove my wife nuts. When settled in to retirement life, I began enjoying the beautiful environment around me, met great people, and made many wonderful friends. To help where I could, I began doing volunteer work in retirement homes across Michigan — betting on the fact I'd reside there myself someday.

2. Lifestyle. I've been busy doing things I'd never done before. Things like studying biology and planting trees on our local golf courses. In particular, I became an advocate for European Beech trees and introduced them to the town — quite fun and very different from performing cataract surgery. As part of my help at retirement homes, I have worked with Tendercare to improve safety for the patients by recommending new equipment and procedures to keep people safe. I also became a coach to my grandson on 35mm photography — go figure.

3. Physical. I have been able to maintain a 12 handicap in golf, which I had during my working days. Since reaching my late-90s, it's creeped up a bit to 14. For the better part of the last twenty-seven retirement years, I played tennis twice a week at the local YMCA. I tried physical fitness, but this isn't for everybody. I gave it up after a couple of very boring sessions.

4. Mental. I read fanatically; books, the "Wall Street Journal" (when the less-than-reliable post office gets it in), and various topical magazines. But I loathed self-help retirement books. Not for me. Those recommended to me were way below my mental capacity and absolutely no fun.

5. *Emotional.* Being one of the founding fathers of Share-Care, a service company for the elderly, and working with them to create care on-demand for retirees was one of the most satisfying and emotional experiences of my life. It's about doing something that makes a difference in people's lives when they grow old and are need of any kind of help. And at 96 years old, I need all the help I can get.

6. *Family and Friends.* My three daughters keep tabs on me from afar, day and night. Maybe it's a good thing that they are more worried about me than I am of myself. They aid me greatly and the visits up here in the cold north are very rich. When you experience the new bond you have it's so surreal and wonderful. And being with the grandkids is a double fantasy — three grandsons and two granddaughters — WOW, a life adventure in itself.

7. *Spiritual.* I've always had a strong faith in God. That will never change, but the last few years I seem to depend on Him a lot more. My family upbringing instilled in me the need to pray constantly and put worries, fears, and grief in the Maker's hands. I guess my grandfather, PopPop, had the biggest influence on me growing up. Not that he put the fear of God in me, but instilled the need to have a strong relationship with Him — or else. My wife's medical problems and her passing a few years back strengthened my beliefs in the hereafter.

8. *Financial.* I started retirement twenty-seven years ago, had a good nest-egg, sold a big house in Toledo for way more than it was worth, and now live in a conservative and moderate small town in Michigan — no financial worries. I think, at 96, my money will outlast me.

William D. Peace, Sr. — Senior Vice President, National Standard Company. Retired October, 1982.

1. Way of Being. All through life we continue to evolve and adapt to the many changes taking place both with the world around us as well as the changes within ourselves. It's no different when you retire. As one ages there comes both physical and mental changes over which you have little or no control, i.e., slowing down physically and experiencing some memory loss for names, etc.

2. Lifestyle. My lifestyle change has allowed me to play more golf and tennis which I have done until age 89+ when I fell and broke my hip. I can still play a little golf (if you call it that now). Now I have more time to read, help where I can, and enjoy family and friends. I have continued to sing in the choir, and occasionally lead the singing at the Rotary Club.

3. Physical. I can better control all my activities. I don't have to rush off to the office, but can enjoy doing things around the house or outside such as yard work, golf, tennis, and countless other things. I love it! If it suits you, get active in the community.

4. Mental. It is most important to keep a positive attitude about life and family/friends. One tends to treasure family and friends much more. It is most important to keep your mind active by being involved with people and community. Keep up with the news — what's going on here and the world, but do not get over upset at the crazy things that happen. It's been that way forever.

5. Emotional. Being with a loving and thoughtful wife has been a tremendous help to keep my emotions relatively calm. I suggest to be more thoughtful and caring; don't let little things crowd out the many wonderful things going on around you. You no longer have work to keep your mind off the disturbing things, so the above really helps.

6. Family and Friends. In your retirement years family and friends become the most important part of your life; especially in avoiding loneliness. Above all, keep active in church, community, and with family/friends.

7. Spiritual. With more time to yourself you contemplate your relationship with the Almighty, His Son and His Spirit. This greatly enhances your entire outlook and attitude. You come to realize how much you need guidance from above. I've been a believer all my life and now I rely on it.

8. Financial. Hopefully, retirees have been planning for later years all their working lives by wisely and carefully investing; saving for the future by building financial resources to continue throughout retirement. It's also wise to study and plan just where you wish to spend your sunset years — nice places, as Bill points out in the book.

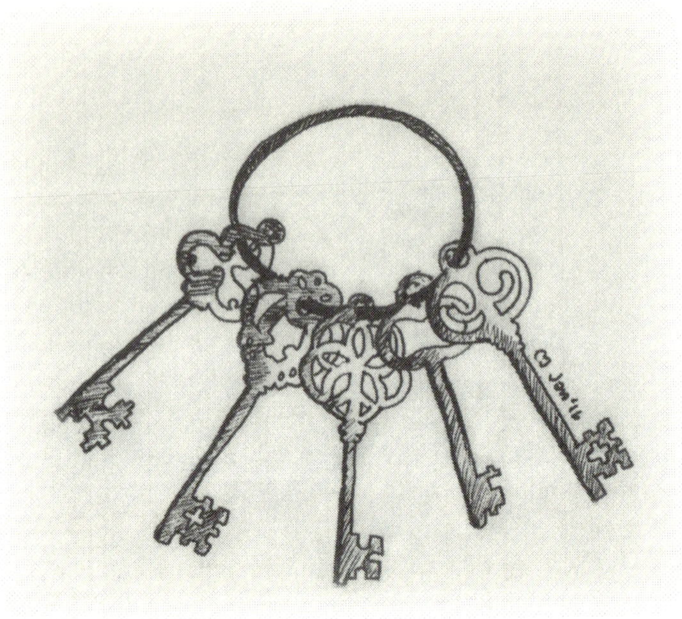

THE MANTRA

As mentioned, living in retirement will mean you will be alone, not lonely, a fair bit of the time. During your work years, being with hundreds of people all the time, all over the world, will mean that this aloneness will take a bit of getting used to. Choose to embrace it, not lament it. I offer up a list of "to-do's" or what you might call a Mantra which can help during your new life. It's like shopping—some clothes will fit, some won't. Try some of these on for size. Alone time and meditation time fits as very useful.

*relax *reflect on your life *internal control vs. external control *what is is, what's so is so what *take care of yourself, take time for yourself *be impeccable with your word, don't take things personally, don't make assumptions, be your best *be/do/have *breathe, listen, be yourself, behave, be with people in a positive way *peace, love, joy, hope *confidence, optimism, positive attitude, enthusiasm (C.O.P.E.) *be strong, brave, tough, wise, present, patient *be gleeful, praising, and rejoice-full *eat well, sleep well, exercise *read, enjoy music *be of good health, take care of your family and friends *it's OK to have a positive ego and high self-esteem.

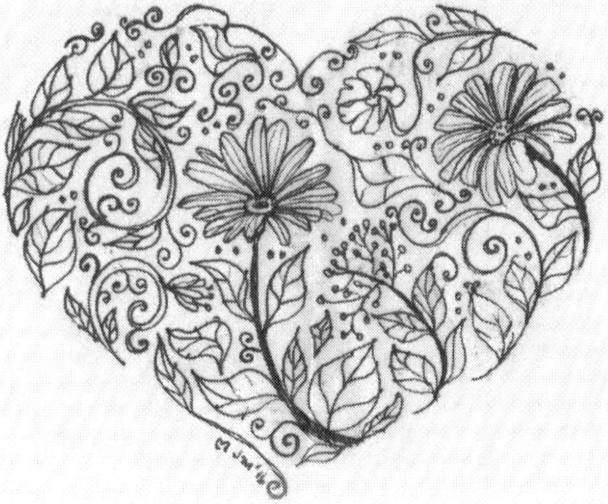

THAT WHICH SAYS IT ALL

When all is said and done, the overarching secret sauce for success in retirement is having a strong faith in God — a living God who carries you in the hard times and walks with you in the good times. What is His guidance? Faith not fear, diligence not worry, health not pain, and righteousness not guilt. A long time ago my mother gave me Max Lucado's daily devotion book, *Grace for the Moment*. (Copyright 2000 by Max Lucado. Published by J. Countryman, Nashville, Tennessee.)

To wrap up this book, I share with you Lucado's take on retirement — that which says it all.

"Growing old can be dangerous. The trail is treacherous and the pitfalls are many. One is wise to be prepared. You know it's coming. It's not like God kept the process a secret. It's not like you are blazing a trail as you grow older. It's not as if no one has ever done it before. Look around you. You have ample opportunity to prepare and ample case studies to consider. If growing old catches you by surprise, don't blame God. He gave you plenty of warning. He also gave you plenty of advice. Your last chapter can be your best. Your final song can be your greatest. It could be that all of your life has prepared you for a grand exit. God's oldest have always been his choicest."

ABOUT THE AUTHOR

William D. Peace Jr. retired from Procter & Gamble in 2007 after 32 years in management positions in North America, Latin America, Western Europe, and Asia. Following retirement, he started up Organizational Management Consulting LLC. He advises companies on supply chain management, logistics, and organizational development. Mr. Peace considers his greatest accomplishment during retirement as being one of the founding fathers of Executives for the Extraordinary, working with the World Vision Foundation of Thailand building schools and libraries in Asia for children in need. When not doing all of this he enjoys time with his three kids, five grandchildren, mom, dad, and sister. He is the author of *Supply Chain Management: The Real WOW Factor,* published in 2011. Mr. Peace resides with his wife, Nathaya Chareon, in Phuket, Thailand, and Leland, Michigan. You can visit him on his website www.omconsultingsite.com to see if he's still living life large. Based on *Retirement: The Surreal Life Adventure,* you gotta get to know this guy and the colleagues he knows who provided the plethora of insights for his book. Have you had a surreal life adventure today? Your S.L.A.?